STUDY GUIDE

The Pilgrim's Progress

A Guided Tour

Derek W. H. Thomas

LIGONIER MINISTRIES

Renew your Mind.

LIGONIER.ORG | 800-435-4343

Copyright © 2013 Ligonier Ministries
421 Ligonier Court, Sanford, FL 32771
E-mail: info@ligonier.org

1

The City of Destruction

MESSAGE INTRODUCTION

John Bunyan's timeless work *Pilgrim's Progress* powerfully expresses the truth that the present life is a spiritual journey. When Jesus Christ liberates a sinner from the power of sin, He also extends an invitation to a lifetime of discipleship. As we shall see, the path of the Christian life is riddled with many trials, dangers, and obstacles. Yet, the journey to the Celestial City is also laden with displays of God's grace and faithfulness. As we begin our study of Bunyan's masterpiece, Dr. Derek Thomas will direct our attention to the City of Destruction, the starting point for Christian's spiritual journey and ours.

SCRIPTURE READINGS

Hebrews 9:27; Psalm 38:4; Acts 16:25-34

TEACHING OBJECTIVES

1. To introduce John Bunyan's classic work *Pilgrim's Progress* and discuss its importance in the lives of generations of Christians.
2. To describe certain events in the early life of John Bunyan that are helpful in understanding this work as his spiritual autobiography.
3. To communicate the burdening nature of sin and the gravity of future judgment.
4. To chronicle the beginning of Christian's spiritual journey, with its ties to Bunyan's experiences and those of believers today.

QUOTATION

Who would true valour see,
Let him come hither;
One here will constant be,
Come wind, come weather.
There's no discouragement

Shall make him once relent
His first avowed intent
To be a pilgrim.

–John Bunyan

LECTURE OUTLINE

I.   The Legacy of *Pilgrim's Progress*

    A. After the Bible, John Bunyan's *Pilgrim's Progress* is the most published book in the history of the English language.

       i.   For many generations, it has been read in Christian homes around the world.

       ii. Many names of characters and locations in Pilgrim's Progress have become common phrases in English literature and everyday speech.

    B. *Pilgrim's Progress* contains two parts.

       i.   Part One, based largely on Bunyan's own experiences, relates Christian's journey to the Celestial City.

       ii. Part Two is the lesser-known story of Christian's wife, Christiana, and their children as they undertake a similar journey.

II. A Man, a Book, and a Burden

    A. *Pilgrim's Progress* begins with a man who is in a state of distress.

       i.   As a resident of the City of Destruction, this man carries a great burden of sin upon his back.

       ii. While reading from a book, this man was awakened to his state of spiritual peril.

    B. This man's conviction of sin parallels Bunyan's own spiritual awakening.

       i.   John Bunyan came of age during the turbulent period surrounding the English Civil War.

       ii. As a young man, he was self-absorbed, vulgar, and hostile to God.

       iii. Through the influence of his wife and others who confronted his sin, Bunyan slowly came to a realization of his need for salvation.

III. Toward the Wicket Gate

    A. Evangelist gave this man direction and encouragement in his state of distress.

       i.   This man, Christian, wanted to escape from judgment but did not know where to go.

       ii. Evangelist instructed Christian to follow a shining light, which would lead him to a wicket gate.

    B. Christian left his family and home behind, covered his ears, and began running toward the light.

    C. Though he could not yet see the gate itself, he was eager to be freed from his burden and spared from the judgment that would befall the City of Destruction.

STUDY QUESTIONS

1. John Bunyan's *Pilgrim's Progress* has furnished the English language with phrases such as By-Path Meadow, Doubting Castle, and Worldly Wiseman.
   a. True
   b. False

2. John Bunyan's father was a _____ by trade.
   a. Farmer
   b. Preacher
   c. Soldier
   d. Tinker

3. Christian became convicted of his sin through _____.
   a. Reading the Bible
   b. The evangelistic efforts of his family and friends
   c. Noticing the burden on his back
   d. The words that Evangelist spoke to him

4. Though his heart had been hostile to God, John Bunyan experienced a sudden conversion as a young man.
   a. True
   b. False

5. Evangelist instructed Christian to go directly to _____.
   a. His home
   b. The foot of the cross
   c. A wicket gate
   d. The Celestial City

BIBLE STUDY AND DISCUSSION QUESTIONS

1. Have you read *Pilgrim's Progress*? If so, what do you recall most vividly about it? If not, what are you most interested in learning from your study of this book?

2. What does it mean to be a pilgrim? Why do you think the metaphor of pilgrimage is a fitting description of the Christian life?

3. What is Christian's situation at the beginning of this story? What needs to change? What is the hope that is extended to Christian and to others in his situation?

4. In this story, does Christian find eternal life immediately or gradually? What truths does this communicate about salvation and the Christian life?

2

The Wicket Gate

MESSAGE INTRODUCTION

When a person becomes aware of his or her sinfulness and need for a savior, he or she may experience a sudden and dramatic spiritual rebirth. Many Christians today and throughout church history have attested to their lives being instantly transformed through an encounter with Jesus Christ. For others, conversion can be a lengthy process, through which Christ gradually draws a sinner to Himself. Such was John Bunyan's experience, and such is the experience of Christian in *Pilgrim's Progress*. In this message, we will witness firsthand the dangers and challenges that Christian faces as he treads the path from conviction of sin toward the Savior's arms.

SCRIPTURE READINGS

Matthew 7:13-14; Matthew 13:1-9, 18-23

TEACHING OBJECTIVES

1. To illustrate the importance of conviction of sin in the process of repentance and faith.
2. To describe many of the spiritual obstacles that people encounter as they come to understand their need for salvation.
3. To warn against the danger of seeking security in one's own good works.
4. To affirm that salvation and peace with God are only possible through the Person and work of Jesus Christ.

QUOTATION

I thought no man in England could please God better than I. But, poor wretch as I was, I was all this while ignorant of Jesus Christ, and going about to establish my own righteousness; and had perished therein, had not God, in mercy, showed me more of my state of nature.

–John Bunyan

LECTURE OUTLINE

I. The Slough of Despond

    A. As Christian made his way toward the wicket gate, two of his neighbors from the City of Destruction overtook him.

        i. Obstinate demonstrates the immovable stubbornness of those who are opposed to the gospel.

        ii. Pliable reveals a fickle readiness to believe anything for a time.

    B. When Obstinate failed to convince Christian to abandon his journey, he returned to the City of Destruction.

    C. For a while, Pliable journeyed alongside Christian.

        i. Pliable was eager to attain a heavenly inheritance, but he was not burdened by a sense of his own sin.

        ii. Pliable was like the seed in Matthew 13:20-21 that responded well initially but never took root.

    D. As they journeyed, Christian and Pliable arrived at the Slough of Despond and began to sink in quicksand.

        i. Because he did not have a burden, Pliable removed himself from the quicksand and returned to the City of Destruction.

        ii. Weighed down by his burden, Christian sank into the quicksand until Help pulled him out.

    E. Help explained that those who bear a burden like Christian's often fall into the Slough of Despond.

        i. Though many had attempted to fill in the slough, it remained just as perilous as ever.

        ii. Nevertheless, the king had constructed stairs in the slough so that pilgrims could find a firm foothold and climb out.

II. The Allure of Morality

    A. As Christian continued toward the wicket gate, he met Mr. Worldly Wiseman.

        i. Seeing Christian's burden, Worldly Wiseman suggested that he visit the village of Morality.

        ii. In Morality there lived a man named Mr. Legality, who was skilled at removing burdens such as the one Christian carried.

        iii. By following the path of moral obedience, Christian could be free from his burden without having to find the wicket gate.

    B. As Christian began to climb the steep hill to Morality, his burden seemed to grow greater and heavier.

    C. Seeing Christian wander from the true path, Evangelist rebuked him and warned him of the danger that awaited him on the path to Morality.

III. Entry through the Gate

    A. Returning to his true path, Christian made his way to the wicket gate.

    B. As he approached the gate, he came within range of arrows being fired from Beelzebub's castle.

C. The gatekeeper, Goodwill, pulled Christian through the gate to safety.
   i. Christian had at last been graciously brought through the wicket gate.
   ii. Though he was on the right path, his burden had not yet been removed.

STUDY QUESTIONS

1. When he failed to deter Christian from his quest, Obstinate _____.
   a. Asked Mr. Worldly Wiseman to distract Christian
   b. Sought consolation in the village of Morality
   c. Convinced Pliable to desert Christian
   d. Returned to the City of Destruction

2. Christian escaped from the Slough of Despond by _____.
   a. Fixing his gaze on the light beyond the wicket gate
   b. Help pulling him out of the quicksand
   c. Finding the steps that the king had placed in the slough
   d. Asking for Mr. Worldly Wiseman's assistance

3. Mr. Worldly Wiseman told Christian that there was a faster and easier way to remove his burden than by following the path to the wicket gate.
   a. True
   b. False

4. What happened when Christian was climbing the steep hill to Morality?
   a. His burden fell off
   b. Evangelist saw his distress and helped him up the hill
   c. Christian's burden seemed heaver than it had been before
   d. Mr. Legality came down the hill to meet Christian

5. Christian avoided Beelzebub's arrows by quickly pulling himself through the wicket gate.
   a. True
   b. False

BIBLE STUDY AND DISCUSSION QUESTIONS

1. How are Obstinate and Pliable different from each other? In what ways are they alike?

2. Where did the Slough of Despond come from, and why could it not be fixed? In what ways do Christians experience the Slough of Despond today? What has God given His people to help them through the slough?

3. What is Christian's burden? What are ways that people, both in Bunyan's story and in actual human experience, try to escape from their burdens? What is needed for a person's burden to be truly removed?

4. As a Calvinist, John Bunyan believed that God is the one who sovereignly and graciously brings sinners to faith in Jesus Christ. How have you noticed God's sovereignty at work in Christian's life? What are some ways that God has displayed His sovereignty in your story of faith?

3

The Interpreter's House

MESSAGE INTRODUCTION

When a person has been awakened to his or her need for a savior, that person also needs to learn about the fundamental realities of the gospel and the Christian life. As Jesus cautioned in Luke 14:27-33, those who decide to follow Him must carefully count the cost of discipleship. Sadly, many professing Christians do not count this cost, and in time they abandon their pilgrimage. In this message, we will join Christian as he learns important lessons about the perils and rewards of a pilgrim's journey.

SCRIPTURE READINGS

Ephesians 6:10-18; Hebrews 6:1-12

TEACHING OBJECTIVES

1. To demonstrate the value of teaching inquirers and new believers about the challenges, complexities, and promises of discipleship.
2. To explain the important spiritual lessons that are conveyed in the different rooms of Interpreter's house.
3. To promote a spirit of humble reliance upon the Person and work of Jesus Christ.
4. To exhort Christ's disciples to work out their salvation with fear and trembling.

QUOTATION

We come tonight to the interpreter's house. And since every minister of the gospel is an interpreter, and every evangelical church is an interpreter's house, let us gather up some of the precious lessons to ministers and to people with which this passage of the Pilgrim's Progress so much abounds.

–Alexander Whyte

LECTURE OUTLINE

I.   The Seven Rooms of Interpreter's House

    A. When Christian entered through the wicket gate, Goodwill directed him to call at the house of Mr. Interpreter.

        i.   Part of the church's mission is to teach inquirers and new believers about the way of salvation and the realities of the Christian life.

        ii. Mr. Interpreter led Christian through his house and showed him spiritual realities that were illustrated in each room.

    B. The first room contained a portrait of a solemn person with a book in his hands and his eyes lifted heavenward.

        i.   This person represents ministers of the gospel who plead with men and women to receive Jesus Christ.

        ii. Christian has already met people like Evangelist, Help, and Goodwill, who demonstrate this calling.

    C. The second room was full of dust, which could only be removed by washing with water.

        i.   Like a broom stirring up dust, the law stirs up an acute awareness of sin.

        ii. Though the law reveals the nature and power of sin, a person can only be cleansed through the gospel.

    D. In the third room were two children, who contrasted the discontent of those who seek fulfillment in this life with the steadfast patience of those who await the life of the world to come.

    E. In the fourth room one man was trying in vain to put out a fire that another man was fueling, illustrating Christ's act, amidst spiritual opposition, of sustaining the flame of the gospel in a person's heart.

    F. A battle raged in the fifth room, in which a man in armor, symbolizing the armor of God in Ephesians 6, vanquished many foes.

    G. The sixth room contained a man in an iron cage.

        i.   This man was once a pilgrim like Christian.

        ii. His heart had become so hardened that he could not repent.

    H. A frightened man in the seventh room had awakened from a dream that depicted God's day of reckoning.

II. A Call to Persevere

    A. The account of the caged man in the sixth room warns believers of the danger of apostasy.

        i.   In the language of Hebrew 6:6, this former pilgrim had despised Jesus Christ and in his heart had crucified him again.

        ii. The true desire of his heart had been for lusts, pleasures, and worldly profit.

    B. Although we rarely hear sermons about apostasy today, the danger of committing the unforgivable sin was frequently addressed in Bunyan's day.

    i. Today, we tend to associate the unforgivable sin simply with the sin of unbelief.

    ii. Yet, many who profess faith in Jesus Christ and believe themselves to be true pilgrims later reveal that their hearts never truly belonged to Christ.

    iii. In this episode, Bunyan reminds Christians, not to doubt God's electing grace, but to closely examine their own hearts and to work out their salvation with fear and trembling.

STUDY QUESTIONS

1. Who instructed Christian to visit Interpreter?
   a. Mr. Worldly Wiseman
   b. Evangelist
   c. Goodwill
   d. Help

2. The dust that was stirred up by the broom in the second room represented
   _____.
   a. The law
   b. Spiritual lethargy
   c. The impatience of this present age
   d. Spiritual warfare

3. Bunyan employed the image of a man secretly fueling a fire to illustrate Christ's act of preserving His saints.
   a. True
   b. False

4. What did Christian see in the sixth room of Interpreter's house?
   a. A man in an iron mask
   b. A scene of the day of judgment
   c. Two children
   d. A man in an iron cage

5. Due to his belief in God's sovereignty, Bunyan did not believe that apostasy was a real danger for professing Christians.
   a. True
   b. False

BIBLE STUDY AND DISCUSSION QUESTIONS

1. What is the significance of Interpreter's house? Why was this an important place for Christian to visit?

2. Which of the rooms in Interpreter's house do you find the most encouraging? How does this room speak to your own experience of the Christian life?

3. Which room in Interpreter's house do you find most sobering or disturbing? What can Christians learn from this room?

4. What does it mean for a professing Christian to apostatize? Does this mean that a Christian has lost his or her salvation? What should believers know about apostasy, and how should they respond to those who forsake their earlier profession of faith?

4

The Cross & the Sepulcher

MESSAGE INTRODUCTION

Many people who have embraced Jesus Christ as Savior and Lord continue to question whether or not they are truly saved. Sometimes this struggle is rooted in intellectual uncertainties. Others may wrestle with their salvation due to the enemy's spiritual attacks or the continued presence of certain sins in their lives. Like many other believers, Christian has continued to be burdened by conviction of his sin. In this message, Dr. Thomas will describe Christian's process of arriving at assurance and examine why it is that Christians can rest upon the saving work of Jesus Christ.

SCRIPTURE READINGS

Zechariah 3:1-5; 2 Corinthians 5:21

TEACHING OBJECTIVES

1. To warn against the potent danger of "Easy-Believism."
2. To articulate the biblical doctrines of justification and imputation.
3. To help Christians to understand and experience assurance of salvation.
4. To encourage God's people to celebrate and delight in Christ's redemptive work.

QUOTATION

Thus far did I come laden with my sin;
Nor could aught ease the grief that I was in
Till I came hither: What a place is this!
Must here be the beginning of my bliss?
Must here the Burden fall from off my back?
Must here the strings that bound it to me crack?
Blest cross! Blest sepulchre! Blest rather be
The Man that there was put to shame for me!

–Christian, free from his burden

LECTURE OUTLINE

I.   Deliverance from the Burden

   A. As Christian left the house of Interpreter, the burden on his back still weighed him down.

   B. After climbing uphill, he came upon a cross with a sepulcher, or tomb, somewhat below it.

      i.   When he reached the cross, the burden upon his back suddenly fell from his shoulders.

      ii. The burden rolled down the hill and disappeared into the sepulcher.

   C. Though this is a joyous moment for Christian, its full significance can be difficult to perceive.

      i.   Many suggest that Christian did not actually become a Christian until he arrived at the cross.

      ii. Others, including Dr. Thomas, believe that Christian became a Christian when he entered at the wicket gate and received assurance of his salvation at the cross.

II. An Alternative to "Easy-Believism"

   A. In Bunyan's day and ours, many people embrace the gospel outwardly without experiencing regeneration and inner communion with Christ.

      i.   "Easy-Believism" encourages sinners to trust in Christ's saving work with little or no regard for his lordship over all of life.

      ii. In contrast, Christian continued to grapple with the reality of his sin even after his sins had been forgiven.

   B. Bunyan reminds his readers of the need to persevere through trials.

III. Assurance of the Great Exchange

   A. As Christian was freed from his burden, three shining beings gave him assurance of his new identity.

      i.   The first declared that Christian's sins had been forgiven.

      ii. The second exchanged Christian's rags for new clothing.

      iii. The third placed a mark upon his forehead and gave him a scroll bearing a seal.

   B. The cross stands as a declaration that Christ has atoned for human sin.

   C. The removal of rags depicts God's act of imputing human sin to Jesus Christ.

      i.   Through His *passive obedience*, Jesus endured the punishment that sinful humanity deserves.

      ii. The Father "made him to be sin who knew no sin" (2 Corinthians 5:21a).

   D. The new clothing represents God's act of imputing the righteousness of Christ to sinners.

      i.   Through His *active obedience*, Jesus earned a righteous status that God requires but humanity cannot attain.

      ii. We are clothed in the obedience of Christ "so that in him we might become the righteousness of God" (2 Corinthians 5:21b).

   E. The sealed scroll is a symbol of Christian's assurance of salvation.

      i. In this scroll, God confirms that Christian's identity is now found in Him.

      ii. Such assurance is a treasure both to be delighted in and to be guarded closely.

STUDY QUESTIONS

1. What happened when Christian reached the cross?
   a. He took off his burden and placed it at the foot of the cross
   b. His burden fell off and disappeared into the nearby tomb
   c. Evangelist explained the gospel and led him in the sinner's prayer
   d. His burden pulled him to the ground, but an angel helped him up

2. Dr. Thomas believes that his arrival at the cross marks Christian's conversion to the Christian faith.
   a. True
   b. False

3. _____ greeted Christian after his experience at the cross.
   a. Three men named Simple, Sloth, and Presumption
   b. The risen Christ
   c. An evil spirit that tempted him
   d. Three shining beings

4. The gifts that Christian received included a _____.
   a. Sealed scroll
   b. Golden ring bearing the king's emblem
   c. Bible
   d. Map of the road ahead

5. God's elect can lose assurance of salvation, but not salvation itself.
   a. True
   b. False

BIBLE STUDY AND DISCUSSION QUESTIONS

1. When did Christian become a Christian? Do you agree or disagree with Dr. Thomas? Why is this timing significant?

2. What is "Easy-Believism?" Why is this approach to faith dangerous? How does John Bunyan address the threat of "Easy-Believism" in *Pilgrim's Progress*?

3. What is the difference between the active obedience of Christ and the passive obedience of Christ? Why are both of these crucial to God's redemptive work?

4. What does it mean to have assurance of salvation? How can a person have such assurance? How can assurance of salvation change a person's life?

5

The Hill Difficulty

MESSAGE INTRODUCTION

Though the Christian journey often contains unique moments of joy and closeness to God, day to day life can challenge a believer's zeal, joy, and sense of purpose. After his powerful arrival at the cross, Christian's journey brings him into contact with people who do not share the same gospel-centered focus that he has. As we turn our attention to this phase in Christian's pilgrimage, we will take note of several dangers and pitfalls that threaten to undermine believers in their spiritual journey.

SCRIPTURE READINGS

2 Corinthians 13:5; Romans 8:28-39

TEACHING OBJECTIVES

1. To warn against the dangers of spiritual apathy and sloth.
2. To emphasize the importance of giving one's heart completely to Christ.
3. To describe the possibility of losing assurance of salvation.
4. To promote among Christians a greater resolve to make their calling and election sure.

QUOTATION

If you have assurance of your justification, do not abuse it. It is abusing assurance when we grow more remiss in duty; as the musician, having money thrown him, leaves off playing. By remissness, or intermitting the exercises of religion, we grieve the Spirit, and that is the way to have an embargo laid upon our spiritual comforts.

–Thomas Watson

LECTURE OUTLINE

I. The Need to Persevere

    A. When Christian left the foot of the cross, he came upon three sleeping men named Simple, Sloth, and Presumption.

    B. When Christian awakened the sleepers and warned them of potential danger, they responded with sleepy indifference.

    C. This interaction illustrates the significance of persevering in the faith.

        i. Christians ought to examine themselves regularly to discern the state of their hearts (2 Corinthians 13:5).

        ii. Yet, Christians can also find rest in God's promise that He will never relinquish His claim on His people (Romans 8:28-39; Philippians 1:6).

II. The Need to Engage the Heart

    A. After leaving Simple, Sloth, and Presumption behind, Christian met two other travelers on the road.

        i. Considering it impractical to enter the road at the wicket gate, these men had climbed over the wall beside the road.

        ii. Formalist and Hypocrisy expressed an interest in saving religion but substituted their own ideas for God's truth.

        iii. As their names and actions indicate, these two men were not true pilgrims.

    B. Formalist possessed a form of godliness but denied its power (2 Timothy 3:5).

        i. Writing in the repressive days of Charles II, Bunyan was imprisoned for defying the religious establishment by preaching without legal authorization.

        ii. In his critique of formalism, Bunyan likely had in mind the complacency of those who participated in the outward rigors of ceremonial religion without a worshipful heart.

    C. While Formalist perhaps had some measure of faith, Hypocrisy did not.

        i. Like many in Bunyan's day and today, Hypocrisy's religiosity was an outward show.

        ii. As Christian suggested, Hypocrisy's true nature would be revealed on the day of judgment.

III. The Need for Continued Assurance

    A. As they walked, Christian, Formalist, and Hypocrisy drew near to a large hill called Difficulty.

    B. Though the other two stayed at the bottom, Christian made his way up the hill until he paused at an arbor built for weary pilgrims.

        i. Christian rested at the arbor and gained encouragement by reading from his scroll.

        ii. Christian drifted off to sleep and awoke several hours later.

    C. Eager to make up for lost time, Christian hastily climbed to the top of the hill before he realized that he had left his assurance scroll behind.

D. In a panic and overcome by guilt and fear, Christian returned to the arbor and recovered his scroll.

STUDY QUESTIONS

1. As he continued on his journey, Christian saw three men named _____.
    a. Pliable, Obstinate, and Presumption
    b. Sloth, Sleep, and Slumber
    c. Laziness, Glutton, and Excess
    d. Simple, Presumption, and Sloth

2. In spite of all his efforts, Christian could not awaken the three sleepers from their slumber.
    a. True
    b. False

3. How did Christian meet Formalist and Hypocrisy?
    a. They were enjoying a lavish feast beside the road
    b. They climbed over the wall and joined him on the road
    c. They saw him struggling to climb the hill and helped him
    d. They had been guests at Interpreter's house

4. Formalist and Hypocrisy tried to persuade Christian to abandon his journey.
    a. True
    b. False

5. What happened when Christian reached the top of the hill?
    a. He sat down and read from his scroll
    b. He fell asleep
    c. He realized that he had lost something of great value
    d. A man named Kindness brought him cool water to drink

BIBLE STUDY AND DISCUSSION QUESTIONS

1. Where did Christian meet the three sleeping men? Why is this surprising? What can we learn from the three sleepers?

2. What was the religious situation in England like during Bunyan's lifetime? How might characters like Formalist and Hypocrisy reflect people that Bunyan would have known? In what ways do these tendencies appear in the church today?

3. What is the significance of the hill known as difficulty? What kinds of hills have you experienced that have challenged you as a Christian?

4. What does Christian's slumber in the arbor represent? How does this sort of spiritual "sleep" affect a person's sense of assurance?

6

The Palace Beautiful

MESSAGE INTRODUCTION

Amidst the challenges and difficulties of the Christian journey, it is important to remember that we are not solitary travelers. After Christian experienced setbacks on the hill Difficulty, his road led him to a place where he found rest, refreshment, and the encouragement of spiritual community. In this message, Dr. Thomas will explain what this segment of Christian's journey can teach us about the church of Jesus Christ and its importance in the lives of God's people.

SCRIPTURE READINGS

Matthew 16:18; Ephesians 2:11-22

TEACHING OBJECTIVES

1. To describe the corporate dimension of the Christian life.
2. To discuss the nature and outcome of the church's spiritual warfare.
3. To express the significance of God-centered fellowship and conversation.
4. To encourage Christians to invest in meaningful relationships with other Christians and to cultivate a greater love for Christ's church.

QUOTATION

Why, there I hope to see Him alive that did hang dead on the cross; and there I hope to be rid of all those things that to this day are in me an annoyance to me: there they say there is no death; and there I shall dwell with such company as I like best. For, to tell you the truth, I love Him because I was by Him eased of my burden; and I am weary of my inward sickness. I would fain be where I shall die no more, and with the company that shall continually cry, 'Holy, holy, holy.'

–Christian

LECTURE OUTLINE

I.   A Place of Beauty

   A. When Christian returned to the top of the hill after finding his lost scroll, he spied a stately palace in the distance and sought shelter there during the night.

   B. In this section, John Bunyan describes the spiritual riches of the church.

      i.   John Calvin is known for proclaiming that a person cannot have God for his father who does not have the church as his mother, a teaching that was articulated by Cyprian in the third century.

      ii. John Bunyan shared a deep love for the church, and he uses this portion of the story to impart to his readers a deeper understanding of the church.

II. Satanic Resistance

   A. Throughout history, the church has been engaged in spiritual warfare.

      i.   On his way to the palace, Christian had to pass by two lions, which had already frightened away the pilgrims Timorous and Mistrust.

      ii. By referring to two lions, Bunyan was perhaps describing the opposition he had experienced both from the state and from the Church of England.

   B. Though Satan's power opposes Christ's disciples, He cannot prevail over them.

      i.   At the palace door, the porter informed Christian that these lions, though fierce, were chained and could not harm him.

      ii. Though the devil may roar and threaten, his power and access are limited.

III. The Gift of Overseers

   A. As the overseer of the palace, the porter represents the elders and ministers through whom Christ governs His church.

   B. When the porter asks Christian about himself, Christian tells the porter of his descent from the line of Japheth.

      i.   Bunyan alludes to Noah's pronouncement in Genesis 9:27.

      ii. Bunyan also draws attention to the spread of the gospel to the Gentiles, a work accomplished through the work of pastors, missionaries, and evangelists (Romans 10:14-15).

   C. As Christian discovered, the church is also a place where believers can share their stories with one another, praising God for His work in their lives.

IV. Spiritual Refreshment

   A. The people of the house enjoyed rich spiritual conversation, which directed Christian's thoughts and feelings toward the king that he was on his way to meet.

   B. Christian also received bodily nourishment, dining upon delicious and rare foods.

   C. In the morning, the people of the house showed Christian a variety of treasures and relics, reminders of the deeds of God's people and of God's faithfulness throughout the ages.

STUDY QUESTIONS

1. In this part of the story, Bunyan uses the imagery of a _____ to describe the church of Jesus Christ.
   a. Flock
   b. Bride
   c. Body
   d. Palace

2. According to Augustine, no one can have God as a father who does not have the church as a mother.
   a. True
   b. False

3. What was unique about the lions at the top of the hill?
   a. They were known for devouring pilgrims
   b. They were restrained by chains
   c. They defended pilgrims from wild beasts
   d. They spoke insults and accusations in human voices

4. What did Christian need to do before he gained entrance to the house?
   a. Share the story of his pilgrimage
   b. Show his scroll as proof that he was a pilgrim
   c. Prove his courage by defeating the lions outside
   d. Nothing; he was granted immediate admittance

5. Within the house, Christian received both physical and spiritual nourishment.
   a. True
   b. False

BIBLE STUDY AND DISCUSSION QUESTIONS

1. What are some examples of the satanic opposition that the church faces today? How can Bunyan's example of the lions outside the palace encourage us amidst such opposition?

2. Why is it important for believers to share their stories with one another? Think of a person whose story of faith you have found particularly encouraging; how did God reveal Himself in that person's life?

3. Christian was asked to answer many questions about his journey. After learning about Christian's failures and shortcomings, how did the people of the house treat him? What can we learn from this, and how can we apply it to our own churches?

4. When Christian was asked why he wanted to go to Mount Zion, what did he say? How can this hope impact our day-to-day lives?

7

The Valley of Humiliation

MESSAGE INTRODUCTION

In the wake of Satan's rebellious struggle against God's rule, Christians do not remain neutral. As soon as a person is united by faith to Jesus Christ, he or she has become a potential target of the Enemy's spiritual attacks. At times these attacks can be direct and apparent, and sometimes they are carried out through subtlety and trickery. By being firmly grounded in the gospel of Jesus Christ and by putting on the full armor of God, Christians can be armed and equipped to withstand the Devil's onslaughts.

SCRIPTURE READINGS

Ephesians 6:10-18; Romans 8:31-39

TEACHING OBJECTIVES

1. To show how the cosmic battle between God and Satan affects believers.
2. To promote a greater awareness of the Devil's weapons and tactics.
3. To encourage Christians to prepare themselves for spiritual battles.
4. To remind pilgrims that in Jesus Christ our battles are already won.

QUOTATION

Grant, Almighty God, since thou hast formerly admonished thy servants, that thy children, while they are pilgrims in this world, must be familiar with horrible and cruel beasts, if the same thing should happen to us, that we may be prepared for all contests. May we endure and overcome all temptations, and may we never doubt thy desire to defend us by thy protection and power, according to thy promise. May we proceed through the midst of numberless dangers, until after accomplishing the course of our warfare, we at length arrive at that happy rest which is laid up for us in heaven by Christ our Lord.

–John Calvin

LECTURE OUTLINE

I. The Parameters of the Battle

    A. After Christian left the Palace Beautiful, he descended the other side of the hill into the Valley of Humiliation.

    B. As he arrived in the valley, a large beast named Apollyon came out to meet him, intent upon destroying him.

    C. The battle between Christian and Apollyon is set within the larger struggle between Jesus and Satan and the kingdom of God against the kingdom of darkness.

        i. Once we are united to Christ, we are subject to affliction and attack from the enemies of Christ.

        ii. As Ephesians 6:13 indicates, the Christian life is characterized by spiritual warfare and by the daily call to take up arms against the forces of evil.

        iii. Christ's disciples periodically experience "evil days" when Satan is on a rampage, unleashing particularly deadly attacks.

II. The Malevolence of the Enemy

    A. Apollyon began by questioning Christian's identity.

        i. Apollyon asserted that Christian was his subject since he was born in the City of Destruction.

        ii. The Devil often tries to remind believers of who they used to be, accusing us of our sins.

    B. Apollyon reminded Christian of his unfaithfulness.

        i. Since Christian claimed to serve a new master, Apollyon drew attention to his shortcomings in serving that master.

        ii. Christian responded wisely by focusing on Christ's forgiveness.

    C. When words failed to deter Christian, Apollyon resorted to force.

        i. He weakened Christian with flaming darts before moving in for close range combat.

        ii. By using his sword and quoting Scripture, Christian warded the enemy off.

III. Resources for Victory

    A. Christian recognized the terrain of spiritual warfare and was firmly grounded in his identity in Christ.

        i. Because Christian knew who he was in Christ, Apollyon could not easily discourage him.

        ii. Similarly, men like Martin Luther and John Bunyan endured temptation and adversity by drawing confidence and strength from their identity in Jesus Christ.

    B. Christian reduced the enemy's strong points.

        i. Apollyon attempted to accuse him of sin.

        ii. Christian disarmed the accusation by confessing that his sins were far greater and that Jesus had already forgiven them.

    C. Christian was clothed in the full armor of God (Ephesians 6:10-18).

STUDY QUESTIONS

1. Apollyon first attacked Christian by questioning his _____.
   a. Identity
   b. Intelligence
   c. Moral record
   d. Knowledge of Scripture

2. When Christian announced that he served a new master, Apollyon claimed that this new master was not worthy of Christian's loyalty.
   a. True
   b. False

3. Apollyon wounded Christian by _____.
   a. Clawing at his unprotected back
   b. Breathing fire at him
   c. Uttering a curse against him
   d. Throwing fiery darts at him

4. Christian defeated Apollyon through the use of Scripture.
   a. True
   b. False

5. Which of the following was not mentioned in this message as a resource for spiritual victory?
   a. Putting on gospel armor
   b. Recognizing the terrain
   c. Using the enemy's weapons against him
   d. Reducing the enemy's strong points

BIBLE STUDY AND DISCUSSION QUESTIONS

1. Where does Apollyon's name come from, and what does it mean? What does he intend to do to Christian?

2. What spiritual battles do you fight in your day-to-day life? How does the enemy most often attack you?

3. How does Dr. Thomas explain the idea of the "evil day" in Ephesians 6:13? What are some examples of "evil days" in the Bible? What moments stand out in your life as particularly evil days or times?

3. Read Ephesian 6:10-18. Which piece of your "armor" is particularly strong? In which area(s) do you need more protection? How can you best prepare yourself to triumph in spiritual battle?

8

The Valley of the Shadow of Death

MESSAGE INTRODUCTION

After Christian left the Valley of Humiliation, his path led him to an even darker and more foreboding place. This is often the case in the Christian life, as one period of difficulty may follow another. In these times, Christians can be particularly vulnerable to temptation, discouragement, and spiritual desolation. Yet, God will not desert His people in the valley. As Christian learned, God's faithfulness often is revealed most poignantly in the midst of doubt and hardship.

SCRIPTURE READINGS

Psalm 23:1-6

TEACHING OBJECTIVES

1. To describe the spiritual dangers of the valley of the shadow of death.
2. To discuss trials and temptations that Christians experience in the valley.
3. To emphasize the need for Christian fellowship during spiritual trials.
4. To encourage Christians to rejoice in God's faithfulness and deliverance from evil.

QUOTATION

Though this valley is thus gloomy, dangerous, mysterious and solitary, yet it is often traversed. Many more go by this road than some people dream. Among those who wear a cheerful countenance in public there are many who are well acquainted with this dreary valley—they have passed through it often—and may be in it now.

–Charles Spurgeon

LECTURE OUTLINE

I.   The Dangers of the Valley

   A.   While one might have expected Christian to enjoy a period of tranquility and rest after his battle against Apollyon, this was not the case.

      i.   As Christian departed the Valley of Humiliation and prepared to follow the road into the Valley of the Shadow of Death, two men ran toward him and urged him to turn around.

      ii.   In spite of the dangers that lay ahead, Christian was determined to reach the Celestial City, even if the road ahead was dangerous.

   B.   Bunyan describes the valley as dark and narrow, marked by the sounds of constant shrieking and howling, and home to hob-goblins, satyrs, and dragons.

   C.   The path through the valley was surrounded by dangers on both sides.

      i.   On the right there was a deep ditch, into which the blind lead the blind (Matthew 15:14).

      ii.   On the left there was a quagmire, out of which a person cannot pull himself (Psalm 69:14).

      iii.   Whenever Christian tried to avoid one of these hazards, he was in danger of stepping into the other.

   D.   The valley does not represent physical death, but spiritual despair.

II.   The Trials of the Valley

   A.   As Christian walked through the valley, an evil creature followed closely behind him and whispered blasphemous thoughts in his ear.

      i.   Not knowing that the creature was there, Christian thought that these blasphemies had come from his own mind.

      ii.   In times of darkness, disciples sometimes experience unwanted thoughts and temptations that seem to come from nowhere.

   B.   The equipment that Christian used to battle Apollyon was of no use in this valley.

      i.   His armor, sword, and shield could not protect him from the darkness or keep him from slipping off the path.

      ii.   The only weapons that Christian could use to ward off the evil creatures around him were Scripture and prayer.

      iii.   The more spiritual our duties and challenges are, the more spiritual our resources need to be.

III. Hope in the Valley

   A.   While he plodded on through the darkness, Christian was encouraged by hearing the voice of Faithful, another pilgrim, ahead of him.

      i.   He realized that others were in the valley and he was not alone.

      ii.   He reasoned that if God had attended to others in the valley, He would attend to him as well.

      iii.   He hoped that he would be able to catch up with him and have companionship on the journey.

B. As the sun began to rise, Christian looked back and saw the dangerous terrain though which God had led him.

C. When he reached the end of the valley, he passed by a cave where two giants had lived for many years, putting to death passing pilgrims.

    i. One giant, Pagan, had been dead for many years; the other, Pope, was no longer capable of harming pilgrims.

    ii. This description expresses Bunyan's hope that, for the seventeenth-century Protestant church, times of persecution and martyrdom were coming to an end.

D. Christian at last left the valley behind him, singing about God's deliverance as he went on his way.

STUDY QUESTIONS

1. The Valley of the Shadow of Death is described in all of the following ways except _____.
    a. As a place of darkness and fear
    b. As a land where many false paths branch off from the true path
    c. As a place where shrieks and howls are heard constantly
    d. As an area where evil and dangerous creatures dwell

2. When Christian tried to avoid the ditch to the right of the path, he was in danger of falling into a quagmire on the left.
    a. True
    b. False

3. What did the evil creature whisper in Christian's ear?
    a. Threatening words
    b. A list of his worst sins
    c. Terrible things that could happen to him
    d. Blasphemies against God

4. Because his sword was of little use in the valley, Christian had to rely upon his shield for protection.
    a. True
    b. False

5. Which of the following ideas did Christian not think of when he heard Faithful's voice ahead of him?
    a. If God kept Faithful safe, He could preserve him as well
    b. He no longer felt alone in the valley
    c. Fighting together, they could defeat the creatures in the valley
    d. He would now have someone to share the journey with

BIBLE STUDY AND DISCUSSION QUESTIONS

1. Describe the Valley of the Shadow of Death in *Pilgrim's Progress*. How might Christians experience this valley in their spiritual lives? How have you experienced the valley?

2. What are some ways that the Devil can launch attacks upon the minds of believers? How can believers withstand these trials of the mind?

3. What words did Faithful utter in the darkness? What can we learn from this?

4. In what ways can the companionship of other Christians help a person to endure the valley? How has God used relationships with other believers to strengthen your faith?

9

The Godless City:
Vanity Fair

MESSAGE INTRODUCTION

Christian has withstood spiritual warfare against the foul Apollyon, and he has safely traversed the Valley of the Shadow of Death. While the dangers behind him were apparent, some dangers are less obvious. Though Vanity Fair may not be known for dark shadows or vicious beasts, its seductive temptations and violent opposition to the king will make it one of the most perilous places that Christian has visited in his travels.

SCRIPTURE READINGS

Proverbs 4:23; John 16:33

TEACHING OBJECTIVES

1. To illustrate the importance of spiritual companionship amidst adversity.
2. To describe the temptation to forsake God in the pursuit of vanity.
3. To discuss ways in which godliness differs from worldliness.
4. To exhort Christians to stand firm in times of trial and persecution.

QUOTATION

Grant, Almighty God, that we may remember ourselves to be pilgrims in the world, and that no splendor of wealth, or power, or worldly wisdom may blind our eyes, but may we always direct our eyes and all our senses towards the kingdom of thy Son. May we always fix them there, and may nothing hinder us from hastening on in the course of our calling, until at length we pass over the course and reach the goal which thou hast set before us.

–John Calvin

LECTURE OUTLINE

I. Christian Camaraderie

    A. Once Christian had emerged from the Valley of the Shadow of Death, he caught up with Faithful, the other pilgrim who had been in the valley.

    B. In Faithful, Christian found much-needed companionship and encouragement for the journey.

        i. There is evidence to suggest that Faithful may represent moderate Anglicans, who would not have experienced the persecution that Bunyan faced.

        ii. The close friendship between Christian and Faithful, in spite of their differences, illustrates the unity and beauty of the church.

    C. As they traversed the countryside, Faithful and Christian were joined by the verbose Talkative.

        i. Though his words were outwardly devout, Talkative revealed a lack of inner maturity and depth.

        ii. Uncomfortable with Christian and Faithful's conversation, Talkative parted ways with them.

    D. The pilgrims were then joined by Evangelist, who warned them of the dangers that awaited them in Vanity Fair.

II. Vanity's Allure

    A. Vanity Fair was a place where pilgrims were tried and tempted.

        i. In ancient times, Apollyon, Beelzebub, and Legion had established this fair on the path to the Celestial City.

        ii. The fair was always open for business, and it sold every kind of good imaginable.

    B. Vanity Fair represents the snare of worldliness.

        i. The things for sale at the fair were not evil, but part of God's good creation.

        ii. Yet, the human heart tends to idolize creation rather than the Creator.

        iii. Instead of loving the world God has made in a God-honoring way, worldliness dismisses God in the pursuit of material goods and pleasures.

    C. Bunyan's depiction of Vanity Fair was not intended to belittle the good things of this life, but to depict the distinction between worldliness and spiritual mindedness in a visual form.

III. A Costly Witness

    A. As Christian and Faithful walked through the fair, they stood out in several ways.

        i. Because their clothing was different, they were viewed as being foolish, insane, and outlandish.

        ii. The heavenly nature of their speech sounded foreign to the ears of the people of the fair.

        iii. They were not interested in purchasing any of the wares that were for sale and even covered their ears to resist the temptation around them.

B. Considered to be troublemakers because they valued truth above the enticements of the fair, the pilgrims were beaten and placed in a cage.
  i. Because of their gracious conduct amidst adversity, many of the towns-people were won over.
  ii. However, the potent witness of these men further enraged most of the townspeople.
C. The leaders of the town brought the pilgrims to trial before Lord Hate-good.
  i. Faithful, who took a vocal stand against the evils of the fair, was accused of violating the ancient laws of the town.
  ii. The jury unanimously found Faithful guilty and put him to death.
D. As Faithful became a martyr, a chariot carried him through the clouds to the celestial gate.

STUDY QUESTIONS

1. After emerging from the Valley of the Shadow of Death, Christian encountered all of the following people except _____.
   a. Goodwill
   b. Evangelist
   c. Talkative
   d. Faithful

2. Why did Christian visit Vanity Fair?
   a. He went there to speak out against the fair's corrupt practices
   b. The king's highway passed through the fair
   c. He was drawn by the allure of worldly goods
   d. The townspeople captured him and took him there against his will

3. Vanity Fair had originally been established by the king and then taken over by the king's enemies.
   a. True
   b. False

4. Which of the following characteristics caused the pilgrims to stand out at Vanity Fair?
   a. The currency that they used
   b. The spiritual weapons that they carried
   c. Their manner of speaking
   d. They were better looking than the others

5. Two pilgrims were brought to trial at Vanity Fair, but only one was executed.
   a. True
   b. False

BIBLE STUDY AND DISCUSSION QUESTIONS

1. According to Dr. Thomas, what kind of person might Faithful represent? Why is this significant, both in Bunyan's day and in our own?

2. What does Vanity Fair represent? Why is this place so dangerous for Christians?

3. Sooner or later, each Christian must travel through Vanity Fair. What wares at the fair are most tempting and alluring to you? What might be good about these things, and how can sin corrupt them? How can you best guard your heart against these temptations?

4. Why did the pilgrims experience such opposition from the people of Vanity Fair? In what ways have you faced spiritual opposition from the people around you?

10

The Castle of Giant Despair

MESSAGE INTRODUCTION

The pilgrimage of the Christian life carries the believer through all types of terrain. After escaping from persecution at Vanity Fair, Christian journeyed onward, sharing the joys and difficulties of the road with Hopeful, a new fellow pilgrim. Choosing to depart from the king's highway in order to follow an easier path, the travellers soon found themselves imprisoned in Doubting Castle, in what constitutes one of the most dark and profound scenes in *Pilgrim's Progress*.

SCRIPTURE READING

Psalm 88:1-18

TEACHING OBJECTIVES

1. To affirm that God is at work in all situations for the good of His people.
2. To discuss certain landmarks on the path to doubt.
3. To dwell upon and wrestle with the anguish of despair and doubt.
4. To encourage God's people to trust in and act upon His promises.

QUOTATION

Darkness and doubts had veiled my mind,
And drowned my head in tears,
Till sovereign grace with shining rays
Dispelled my gloomy fears.

–Isaac Watts

LECTURE OUTLINE

I. The Road to Doubting Castle

    A. After Christian escaped from Vanity Fair, he was joined by a man named Hopeful.

        i. Hopeful had observed the martyrdom of Faithful and by it was persuaded to become a pilgrim himself.

      ii.   Throughout the remainder of their journey, Hopeful and Christian will form a close friendship, benefitting greatly from one another's company.

   B. A man named Mr. By-Ends asked to join the pilgrims on their journey.

      i.   By-Ends, who came from the town of Fair-speech, placed a high value on wealth and social standing.

      ii.   Christian warned By-Ends that in order to join them he would need to renounce his love for popularity and profit.

      iii. As they left him behind, By-Ends found fitting companions in Mr. Hold-the-world, Mr. Money-love, and Mr. Save-all.

   C. After walking for several more days and enjoying ease of travel, the path became more difficult.

      i.   At By-path Meadow they stepped over the fence to an adjacent path that was easier to walk upon and appeared to lead in the same direction.

      ii.   When night came, they realized that they had strayed significantly from their true course.

II. Captives of Despair

   A. The pilgrims had wandered onto the land of the giant Despair, who took them to Doubting Castle as his prisoners.

      i.   This dungeon is a sinister place, representing the spiritual darkness described in Psalm 88.

      ii.   They remained in Despair's dungeon from Wednesday morning until Saturday night, likely alluding to the period of Jesus' suffering and death.

   B. The giant treated the pilgrims harshly and urged them to end their misery by taking their own lives.

      i.   Christian was tempted to follow the giant's advice, but Hopeful persuaded him to await God's deliverance.

      ii.   When the giant returned to check on the pilgrims, he was furious that they were still alive.

   C. Every day the giant tried harder to break their spirits and prompt them to abandon life.

III. Escape from Doubt

   A. After days of captivity, Christian and Hopeful began to pray on Saturday night and continued praying until morning had nearly come.

   B. Shortly before daybreak, Christian suddenly recalled that he had been given a key called Promise.

      i.   Using this key, Christian unlocked the doors that had previously barred their escape.

      ii.   By the time the giant was aware of what they were doing, the pilgrims had already left the castle.

   C. When they returned to the king's highway, they set up a sign to warn other travellers of the danger.

STUDY QUESTIONS

1. Hopeful decided to join Christian on his journey after _____.
   a. Christian warned him of the wrath that was to come
   b. He watched Faithful give his life for his faith while in Vanity Fair
   c. Evangelist told him about the road to the Celestial City
   d. He became aware of a burden on his back and wanted to be free

2. The pilgrims departed from the king's highway because it looked like it would be easier to walk on the other side of the fence.
   a. True
   b. False

3. What did the giant Despair urge Christian and Hopeful to do?
   a. Take their own lives
   b. Pay him a sizeable ransom in exchange for their freedom
   c. Renounce their loyalty to the king and serve him instead
   d. Turn against each other

4. As soon as Christian began to pray, he remembered that he had a key that could open the prison door.
   a. True
   b. False

5. When Christian and Hopeful returned to the king's highway, they _____.
   a. Destroyed the stile so that no one else could cross over the fence
   b. Made plans to return to the castle and destroy it
   c. Built a wall to keep the giant away from the highway
   d. Set up a sign to warn other pilgrims of the danger

BIBLE STUDY AND DISCUSSION QUESTIONS

1. Describe Mr. By-Ends. What prevented him from joining Christian and Hopeful? How does Mr. By-Ends serve as a warning for believers today?

2. How did the pilgrims wander onto the giant's estate? In what way might this situation have been avoided?

3. Think about a time of doubt or despair in your life. In what ways was your experience similar to or different from Christian and Hopeful's imprisonment? How has this time influenced your journey of faith?

4. What was special about the key that Christian had? How can this key unlock prison doors in your life?

11

The Delectable Mountains

MESSAGE INTRODUCTION

Though God's people are often called to walk difficult paths, God is faithful to supply moments of rest in order to strengthen and sustain His pilgrims. After enduring numerous hardships and trials, Christian and Hopeful at last arrive in the Delectable Mountains, a place of safety and spiritual refreshment. As they prepare for the final phase of their journey, the shepherds of the mountains equip the pilgrims with both encouragement and clear warnings of the dangers that still confront them.

SCRIPTURE READING

Psalm 84:1-12

TEACHING OBJECTIVES

1. To commend the Lord's Day as much-needed "market day of the soul."
2. To affirm the importance of God-honoring leadership.
3. To warn professing Christians of the danger of apostasy.
4. To encourage Christians to seek glimpses of the heavenly city in the life of the church.

QUOTATION

O Lord most high, O God eternal, all whose works are glorious, and whose thoughts are very deep: there can be no better thing than to praise thy name and to declare thy loving-kindness in the morning, on thy holy and blessed Sabbath day!

–Lewis Bayly

LECTURE OUTLINE

I. The Pattern of the Lord's Day

    A. Having safely returned to the true path, Christian and Hopeful arrived at the Delectable Mountains.

       i.   Christian had seen these mountains in the distance when he was at the Palace Beautiful.

      ii.   These mountains belonged to the king, and from them a person could see the gate of the Celestial City.

     iii.   Though some suggest that these mountains represent spiritual maturity, there is also reason to suppose that Bunyan is once more describing the church and the blessings that come to God's people through the church.

B. As was the case with most of the Puritans, the Lord's Day occupied an important place in Bunyan's theology.

       i.   Following the Sabbath pattern of the Old Testament, the Puritans emphasized the importance of setting apart one day in seven for the worship of God.

      ii.   John Geree described this day as a "market day of the soul," when a person could obtain much-needed spiritual nourishment.

     iii.   Rather than thinking of the Lord's Day as a burden, the Puritans considered it a day to be anticipated and enjoyed.

II. The Provision of Godly Leaders

A. As they ascended the Delectable Mountains, Christian and Hopeful met four shepherds named Knowledge, Experience, Watchful, and Sincere.

B. As they fed the flock, these shepherds explained to the pilgrims that the sheep belonged to Emmanuel and that he laid down His life for them.

       i.   Though the sheep belonged to the king, it was the responsibility of the shepherds to feed and protect them.

      ii.   As a pastor, Bunyan was deeply aware of the importance of Godly leadership in the church.

III. The Perseverance of the Saints

A. Throughout Christian's journey, there have been numerous warnings about the perils that await unwary pilgrims.

B. The shepherds led Christian and Hopeful to the top of a hill called Error.

       i.   The hill sloped gradually upward on one side, but there was a steep cliff on the other side where others had fallen.

      ii.   This hill was a warning against those who, like Hymenaeus and Philetus, were in danger of forsaking the gospel by falling into error (2 Timothy 2:17-18).

C. The shepherds then led the pilgrims to the top of a hill called Caution, where they could see other travelers who had been captured and blinded by Giant Despair.

D. The shepherd showed them a door in the hillside which led directly to Hell.

       i.   Even travelers who had completed most of the journey to the Celestial City had passed through this door and on to judgment.

      ii.   Once more, Bunyan is warning his readers of the danger of making a false profession of faith and of showing outer signs of piety without having truly been born again.

E. After seeing these grave warnings, Christian and Hopeful also saw something which gave them hope.
    i.   Looking through the perspective glass, they beheld in the distance the gate of the Celestial City.
    ii. A glorious hope awaits those who persevere in their pilgrimage of faith.

STUDY QUESTIONS

1. According to Dr. Thomas, the Delectable Mountains most likely describe _____.
    a. Excitement shared by new Christians
    b. The experiences of mature believers
    c. Moments of heightened spiritual joy
    d. The blessings that come through the church

2. Although most Puritans considered Sabbath observance to be a burden, John Bunyan believed the Lord's Day was something to be enjoyed.
    a. True
    b. False

3. What were the shepherds doing when Christian and Hopeful met them?
    a. They were telling stories about unwary travelers
    b. They were feeding the sheep that were under their care
    c. They had left the flock behind in order to search for one lost sheep
    d. They were defending their sheep against a wild beast

4. The hill called Error was so steep that no one could climb to the top of it.
    a. True
    b. False

5. From the top of the hill Caution, Christian and Hopeful could see _____.
    a. Blind men stumbling around
    b. The bones of pilgrims who had fallen from the top
    c. The gates of the Celestial City
    d. Smoke rising from the City of Destruction

BIBLE STUDY AND DISCUSSION QUESTIONS

1. In Bunyan's allegory, what do you think the Delectable Mountains describe? Why is this a good comparison?

2. What does it mean to describe the Lord's Day as "the market day of the soul?" From which spiritual goods and delicacies does your soul most benefit on the Lord's Day?

3. The names of the shepherds of the Delectable Mountains are Knowledge, Experience, Watchful, and Sincere. Consider these attributes; why is each of these qualities important in a shepherd or leader?

4. As Christian and Hopeful journeyed through the Delectable Mountains, they were able to catch a glimpse of the Celestial City. In what ways have you experienced a foretaste of God's heavenly city in your interactions with other believers?

12

The Celestial City

MESSAGE INTRODUCTION

Eventually, each Christian's pilgrimage in this world will come to an end. As Christian and Hopeful discover, the end of the journey brings with it a variety of emotions and experiences. Just as each believer's life is different, so also each Christian's departure from this life is different. Yet, the anticipation of the Celestial City is something that all true pilgrims can share, as fear of death gives way to the joy of entering the King's presence.

SCRIPTURE READINGS

Isaiah 43:1-7; Revelation 19:1-9

TEACHING OBJECTIVES

1. To describe the glorious experience of entering the Celestial City.
2. To emphasize the necessity of faith in Jesus Christ for salvation.
3. To remind Christ's followers that they do not need to fear death.
4. To encourage Christians to prepare themselves for their eventual death, so that they might live well and die well.

QUOTATION

"You are going now to the paradise of God, wherein you shall see the tree of life, and eat of the never-fading fruits thereof: and when you come there you shall have white robes given you, and your walk and talk shall be every day with the King, even all the days of eternity."

–The shining ones, addressing Christian and Hopeful

LECTURE OUTLINE

I. The River of Death and Life Everlasting

   A. Having left the Delectable Mountains, Christian and Hopeful passed through Enchanted Ground and made their way to the land of Beulah.

      i. Beulah land was a place of safety, far beyond the reach of the villains and monsters that the pilgrims had encountered.

      ii. Beulah land was a place of wonders and delights, where the pilgrims enjoyed exquisite food and drink from the king's gardens and vineyards.

B. The pilgrims met two shining ones, who traveled with them to the River of Death that stood between them and the gate to the Celestial City.

      i. They could not enter the city unless they passed through the river.

      ii. The river appeared to be deep, and there was no bridge over it.

C. Intent upon reaching the city, the pilgrims entered the river.

      i. Christian began to sink down into the water and thought he was going to drown.

      ii. Hopeful could feel the bottom of the river, and he walked through the water without fear.

      iii. Hopeful held Christian's head above the water, and the two of them gradually made their way to the other side of the river.

D. Christian and Hopeful at last entered the Celestial City.

      i. At the king's order, the gates were opened for them.

      ii. Since their mortal garments were left in the river, they were given new heavenly garments to wear.

      iii. The pilgrims were welcomed by feasting and rejoicing.

II. The Reality of Death

A. Readers of *Pilgrim's Progress* in the twenty-first century are not as familiar with death as people were in Bunyan's day.

      i. Many of Bunyan's readers, like Bunyan himself, had experienced the loss of loved ones.

      ii. *Pilgrim's Progress* assures Christians that for those who trust in Christ death should hold no fear.

B. Christians do not all experience the process of dying in the same way.

      i. For some, like Christian, faith and assurance may waver in the face of death.

      ii. Others, like Hopeful, demonstrate strong faith at the time of death.

III. Preparation for Death

A. Bunyan and other Puritans such as Thomas Goodwin encouraged their flock to think about death and be prepared for it.

B. Because a person does not receive a second chance, it is important to die well and to be prepared to meet God at the moment of death.

STUDY QUESTIONS

1. Christian and Hopeful encountered all except _____ in Beulah land.

    a. Lush gardens and vineyards

    b. Wicked monsters making trouble for pilgrims

    c. Extravagant feasting and celebration

    d. Shining citizens of the Celestial City

2. Knowing that the road ahead was perilous, the pilgrims spent several days in Beulah land in order to rest and prepare themselves.
    a. True
    b. False

3. The shining ones told Christian and hopeful to cross the river by _____.
    a. Walking on the water through faith
    b. Purchasing passage on the boat called *Gospel Truth*
    c. Descending into the water and going through the river
    d. Finding a bridge that was farther downstream

4. Because Hopeful was a less experienced pilgrim, Christian had to help him across the river.
    a. True
    b. False

5. As the pilgrims reached the end of their journey, what happened to their traveling clothes?
    a. Their clothing was miraculously transfigured
    b. They had to wash their clothes thoroughly before entering the city
    c. They were given shining robes to cover up their traveling clothes
    d. They were given new clothes to replace their old clothes

BIBLE STUDY AND DISCUSSION QUESTIONS

1. Interestingly, Bunyan does not end the story with Christian and Hopeful. Instead, he describes a man named Ignorance attempting to enter the Celestial City. What happened to Ignorance? What do you think Bunyan is trying to communicate?

2. Christian and Hopeful responded to the River of Death very differently. Do you more easily identify with Christian or with Hopeful? Explain your answer.

3. As the pilgrims crossed the river, Hopeful's feet could touch the bottom, but Christian's could not. How are we to understand this difference?

4. As you think about your own future death, what thoughts and feelings come to mind? What does it mean to be prepared for death, and how can you prepare yourself for it?

13

A New Journey Begins

MESSAGE INTRODUCTION

After a follower of Jesus has departed from this life, God may continue to use his or her influence to change the lives of others. Even those whose hearts were once hardened against the gospel can later be softened by the memory of a believer's testimony and the regenerating work of the Holy Spirit. In this message, we will turn our attention to the wife and children that Christian left behind when he began his pilgrimage to the Celestial City. Though they were once hostile to Christian's faith, their attitudes have changed since his departure.

SCRIPTURE READING

Ezekiel 37:1-14

TEACHING OBJECTIVES

1. To introduce the second part of Bunyan's *Pilgrim's Progress*.
2. To compare and contrast the two parts of the story.
3. To describe Christiana's decision to become a pilgrim.
4. To promote a greater appreciation for the ways that God works within families.

QUOTATION

Go, then, I say, tell all men who thou art:
Say, I am Christiana; and my part
Is now, with my four sons, to tell you what
It is for men to take a Pilgrim's lot.

–John Bunyan

LECTURE OUTLINE

I. A Continuing Story

    A. John Bunyan completed the first part of Pilgrim's Progress in 1678.

        i.   Published with the assistance of John Owen, this book enjoyed immense popularity.

        ii. In the years that followed, several other people attempted to write a sequel to Bunyan's work.

    B. In 1684, Bunyan himself published the story of Christian's wife and children as the continuation of his original story.

    C. Part two begins as a conversation in which the narrator asks Mr. Sagacity to tell him about what happened to Christian.

        i.   It is learned that Christian dwells contentedly in the Celestial City, enjoying great honor and daily fellowship with the king.

        ii. The conversation then turns to Christian's wife and children.

II. A Gospel Story

    A. As a Puritan, Bunyan's beliefs and writings were shaped profoundly by the gospel of Jesus Christ.

        i.   In Christ's atoning death, punishment for human sin was diverted to Him.

        ii.   By faith, sinners are declared just before God and are clothed in Christ's righteousness.

        iii. Faith in Christ is a gift.

    B. Mr. Sagacity informs the narrator that Christian's wife, Christiana, had begun a pilgrimage of her own.

        i.   Although she had initially dismissed her husband as insane, her heart gradually changed toward him and his beliefs.

        ii. At last, she received an invitation to faith and responded to God's effectual call.

III. A Road Story

    A. Like part one, part two is a story about pilgrimage.

    B. This story is rooted in biblical imagery about the Christian life, especially Luke's description of Christianity as "the way."

    C. Following in Christian's footsteps, Christiana and her sons leave the City of Destruction in pursuit of a better city.

IV. A Family Story

    A. The focus in part two is not on an individual traveler, but on a family of believers.

        i.   In this story, Bunyan emphasizes the importance of religion within the context of the family.

ii. Women play a significant role within this story, as Bunyan highlights the relationship between a mother and her children.

V. An Adventure Story

A. Christiana will encounter a variety of diverse characters and will face many challenging situations.

B. Like part one, there are many examples of courage and perseverance.

C. In contrast to part one, Bunyan introduces weak characters, such as Mercy, who will withstand trials and accomplish heroic things in spite of their initial weakness of faith.

STUDY QUESTIONS

1. John Bunyan published parts one and two as two separate books before publishing both in a single volume the following year.
    a. True
    b. False

2. As Bunyan begins the second part of the story, _____ brings the reader up to date with the recent experiences of Christian and his family.
    a. Mr. Sagacity
    b. The unnamed narrator
    c. Evangelist
    d. The martyred and resurrected Faithful

3. What finally prompted Christiana to leave the City of Destruction?
    a. She had a vision of an angel bringing punishment upon the city
    b. She began to read the same book that Christian had read
    c. She received a personal invitation from the Merciful One
    d. She became very lonely and longed to be with her husband

4. Dr. Thomas describes the story of Christiana and the boys in all of the following ways except as _____.
    a. A family story
    b. A love story
    c. An adventure story
    d. A gospel story

5. In part two, Bunyan devotes greater attention to spiritual weakness than he did in part one.
    a. True
    b. False

BIBLE STUDY AND DISCUSSION QUESTIONS

1. What are some of the reasons that few people have read the second part of *Pilgrim's Progress*? Based on the overview given in this message, what are some of the major differences between part one of *Pilgrim's Progress* and part two?

2. How has the first part of this study impacted you? What are your expectations for the second part of our study?

3. The story of Christiana and the boys illustrates the way that God can bring spiritual life to an entire family, even though some family members may initially show great resistance to the gospel. In this case, do you most identify with Christian, Christiana, or their children? Explain your answer.

4. Christiana's decision to become a pilgrim did not come about quickly. Describe the process of heart change that she experienced. How does this compare with your own story and the stories of others that you know?

14

Foes & Friends: The Road to Interpreter's House

MESSAGE INTRODUCTION

Some dangers in life are apparent, and others are not. As Christiana and her companions approached the wicket gate, they encountered unexpected opposition from the forces of darkness. In all ages, pilgrims need to remain vigilant and sober-minded even when things seem to be going well. Like Christiana, believers today benefit from the lessons and warnings that are found in the interpreter's house.

SCRIPTURE READING

Matthew 5:1-11

TEACHING OBJECTIVES

1. To describe the dangers that the pilgrims encountered near the gate.
2. To remind Christians of the need to be prepared for opposition.
3. To present important lessons about the Christian life.
4. To rejoice in God's mercy to the meek and poor in spirit.

QUOTATION

"As my Lord sees, I am come. And if there is any grace and forgiveness of sins to spare, I beseech that thy poor handmaid may be a partaker thereof."

–Mercy, standing at the wicket gate

LECTURE OUTLINE

I. Satanic Opposition to Faith

  A. The Devil will do His utmost to harm those who are intent on coming to Christ.

    i. As Christiana knocked at the wicket gate, a large dog began to bark.

      ii. When Christiana and her sons had entered, their companion Mercy was left alone outside.

      iii. Mercy acknowledged her unworthiness and her weakness of faith, and the gatekeeper pulled her to safety.

      iv. The gatekeeper told the pilgrims that the dog belonged to Beelzebub and often came around to hinder pilgrims from entering the wicket gate.

  B. Pilgrims do not have because they do not ask (Matthew 7:7-12; James 4:2).

      i. As Christiana and her companions continued their journey, they were attacked by two ruffians and were nearly overcome.

      ii. Reliever came to the aid of the women, and the ill-favored ruffians fled over the fence.

         1. Reliever told the group that the gatekeeper would have sent someone to escort them if they had asked.

         2. Because they did not ask, they did not receive.

  C. Pilgrims should not let the blessings of the journey distract them from the dangers of the road.

      i. In response to Reliever, Christiana replied that the blessing of entering through the gate had distracted them from the need to be prepared for trouble.

      ii. When things appear to be going well, Christians ought to be on their guard.

II. Seven lessons at Interpreter's House

  A. When the pilgrims arrived at Interpreter's House, they were first shown a man raking leaves and twigs, oblivious to the golden crown above him.

  B. Although the second room was neat and tidy, it was home to a spider.

  C. The third room contained chickens, which raised their heads to heaven after each sip of water that they drank.

  D. In the fourth room a butcher was killing a sheep, which remained silent and calm in the face of trouble.

  E. Next they saw a garden in which many different flowers grew without struggle or discord.

  F. Finally, they watched a small robin eat worms and spiders, representing professing Christians who secretly feed upon sin.

III. Grace for the Unworthy

  A. As they awaited their meal, they spoke of spiritual things.

  B. Though timid and unsure of herself, Mercy shared her testimony with the others.

      i. Though not outwardly courageous, Mercy demonstrated a spirit of gentleness and humility.

      ii. Mercy's acute awareness of her own frailty and unworthiness made her a grateful recipient of God's grace.

STUDY QUESTIONS

1. The dog that the pilgrims encountered near the wicket gate belonged to
   _____.
   a. Apollyon
   b. The gatekeeper
   c. Beelzebub
   d. Giant Despair

2. The gatekeeper did not provide an escort for Christiana because she did not ask for one.
   a. True
   b. False

3. What else was in the room with the man who was using a rake?
   a. A crown
   b. A spider
   c. Chickens
   d. A robin

4. Interpreter showed the pilgrims a garden full of flowers with all the tops cut off.
   a. True
   b. False

5. After Mercy shared her testimony at Interpreter's home, _____.
   a. She wished that she had remained silent
   b. Interpreter was puzzled that she had been admitted at the gate
   c. Christiana began to regret bringing Mercy with her
   d. She went to bed with God's praise on her lips

BIBLE STUDY AND DISCUSSION QUESTIONS

1. Why did the dog bother the travelers? What "dogs" in your life can prevent you from bringing your needs to Jesus?

2. As she focused on the blessings of her journey, Christiana was not alert to potential dangers. In what ways do you tend to let your spiritual guard down when all seems well?

3. Interpreter did not show Christiana the same rooms that he showed Christian. Why do you think that is? What does that suggest about a minister of the gospel?

4. What was significant about the robin that the pilgrims saw? What kind of warning does the robin represent for Christians today?

15

The Trek to the Palace

MESSAGE INTRODUCTION

Though no two Christians have identical spiritual biographies, there are often points of similarity in the stories and experiences of believers. As Christiana, Mercy, and the children follow the same route that Christian walked earlier, they continue to encounter many of the same people and landmarks on their way to the Palace Beautiful. By describing numerous changes and developments that have taken place since Christian's journey, Bunyan conveys important insights about the life of a pilgrim.

SCRIPTURE READING

Philippians 3:13-14

TEACHING OBJECTIVES

1. To elaborate upon several of the brief incidents recorded in part one.
2. To emphasize the importance of sound doctrine for spiritual warfare.
3. To remind Christians to remain spiritually alert in difficult times.
4. To exhort Christians to present their requests boldly to God.

QUOTATION

"These women and children are going on pilgrimage, and this is the way they must go; and go it they shall, in spite of thee and the lions."

–Great-heart, addressing Grim the giant

LECTURE OUTLINE

I. Up the Hill

    A. Interpreter sent Mr. Great-heart to accompany the pilgrims to the Palace Beautiful.

        i. Bearing weapons and armor, Great-heart was prepared to protect the women and children from enemies and perils.

        ii. As they walked, Great-heart explained important doctrines like Chalcedonian Christology and the substitutionary work of Christ.

    B. As they followed the king's highway, Great-heart pointed out many of the same people and places that Christian had encountered on his pilgrimage.

        i. The bodies of the former sleepers—Simple, Sloth, and Presumption—hung beside the road as a warning to others.

        ii. At the foot of the hill Difficulty, the spring where Christian had found refreshment had since been contaminated by the king's enemies.

        iii. The false paths that Formality and Hypocrisy had followed had been blocked off, but they were still taken by travelers who did not want to ascend the hill.

    C. Halfway up the hill, the travelers stopped at the prince's arbor to rest.

        i. Learning from Christian's misfortune, they did not fall asleep.

        ii. They feasted upon some of the provisions that Interpreter had sent.

        iii. Just as Christian had lost his scroll at that arbor, Christiana lost a bottle of spirits at the same place.

II. At the Hilltop

    A. As the pilgrims drew near to the palace, they had to contend with the same lions that had frightened Christian.

        i. The grass had begun to grow thick, indicating that few pilgrims had passed near the lions recently.

        ii. Since the lions represent the powers of church and state, this is likely Bunyan's commentary on the heightened religious persecution that took place during the 1680s.

    B. Though the lions themselves were chained, an evil giant named Grim barred the pilgrims' path.

        i. Also known as "Bloody-man," Grim had a reputation for killing pilgrims.

        ii. Great-heart drew his sword and killed Grim in battle.

    C. Once Grim had been slain, the pilgrims made their way safely past the lions to the Palace Beautiful.

    D. Like Christian before them, Christiana and her companions enjoyed excellent physical and spiritual nourishment inside the Palace Beautiful.

STUDY QUESTIONS

1. Because Great-heart was skilled in spiritual warfare, he saw little use for theological knowledge.
   a. True
   b. False

2. Christiana discovered that Simple, Sloth, and Presumption _____.
   a. Were dead
   b. Had decided to go to the Celestial City
   c. Were still asleep
   d. Had gone to live in Vanity Fair

3. What happened when the pilgrims paused at the arbor on the hill?
   a. They fell asleep
   b. They set up a sign to warn others not to sleep
   c. They ate and continued their journey
   d. Christiana lost her scroll

4. When the pilgrims drew near to the lions, they noticed that _____.
   a. There were now three lions
   b. Other pilgrims had not been that way lately
   c. The lions had broken free of their chains
   d. Someone had slain the lions

5. After Great-heart killed the giant, the pilgrims proceeded safely to the Palace Beautiful.
   a. True
   b. False

BIBLE STUDY AND DISCUSSION QUESTIONS

1. Describe Great-heart. In what ways did he assist the pilgrims on their journey to the Palace Beautiful?

2. What did Great-heart and Christiana discuss as they set out from Interpreter's home? In light of the fact that Great-heart's armaments included knowledge of these topics, how can we prepare for spiritual warfare?

3. What happened to both Christian and Christiana on their way up the hill Difficulty? What danger does this represent for your own experiences of difficulty?

4. Great-heart returned to Interpreter because the pilgrims had not asked him to stay with them earlier. Similarly, Christians do not always ask God for things that are important to them. What requests do you hesitate to bring before God? How might you have missed out on God's blessings as a result?

16

The Road to Vanity & Vanity Fair

MESSAGE INTRODUCTION

Though we do not know what the road ahead of us may hold, God's pilgrims can be confident that He knows their needs. During a long stay at the Palace Beautiful, Christiana and her fellow travelers find much-needed respite from their journey. When the time comes for them to resume their travels, they are joined by traveling companions whose presence is an aid in times of darkness and danger. As they follow the king's highway, their troupe continues to grow as they experience new joys and challenges.

SCRIPTURE READINGS

Proverbs 3:5-6; Isaiah 50:10

TEACHING OBJECTIVES

1. To describe the spiritual healing and refreshment found in the church.
2. To emphasize the importance of prayer.
3. To encourage Christians in dark places to place their hope in Christ.
4. To foster a greater love for Christian community and fellowship.

QUOTATION

"I have heard much of your husband, and of his travels and wars which he underwent in his days. Be it spoken to your comfort, the name of your husband rings all over these parts of the world: his faith, his courage, his enduring, and his sincerity under all, had made his name famous."

–Mr. Honest, addressing Christiana

LECTURE OUTLINE

I. Respite at the Palace

    A. Christiana and her companions remained at the Palace Beautiful for about a month.

    B. The attractive and industrious Mercy succeeded in warding off unwanted attention from a man named Mr. Brisk.

    C. One of the boys received treatment for a grave illness.

        i. He had climbed the fence and eaten some fruit from a tree that grew on Beelzebub's land.

        ii. A physician named Mr. Skill prescribed the use of the potion *ex carne et sanguine Christi* ("from the body and blood of Christ") in order to heal him.

    D. Once they were ready to resume their journey, Christiana sent a request to Mr. Interpreter, asking that he allow Great-heart to be their escort for the remainder of the pilgrimage.

II. The Path through the Valleys

    A. As the travelers made their way to the Valley of Humiliation, they heard the sound of birds singing lines from the Psalms.

    B. Upon entering the Valley of Humiliation, they saw a monument commemorating Christian's battle against Apollyon.

        i. They could see Christian's bloodstains on the ground and Apollyon's broken arrows lying nearby.

        ii. They also learned that the king had spent time in this valley and that pilgrims had met with angels in the valley.

    C. In the Valley of the Shadow of Death, they encountered heightened spiritual opposition.

        i. As they walked through the darkness, they caught frequent glimpses of evil creatures.

        ii. They had to proceed cautiously in order to avoid falling into pits and being caught in snares.

        iii. Near the end of the valley, they were attacked by a giant named Maul.

        iv. Great-heart killed the giant, and the pilgrims left the valley.

III. The Road to Gaius' Inn

    A. When they reached the place where Christian had met Faithful on his journey, they met a man named Mr. Honest.

        i. Mr. Honest joined them in their travels and offered them encouragement.

        ii. They discussed pilgrims that had gone before, including Mr. Fearing, who reached the Celestial City in spite of his imperfection and weak faith.

    B. Mr. Honest led them to an inn owned by a man named Gaius, who loved the king and frequently sheltered weary pilgrims.

IV. Refreshment at the Inn

   A. Gaius' inn is another representation of the blessings that Christ gives His followers through the church.

   B. Great-heart and Gaius searched for the brutal giant Slay-good, killed him, and rescued the fearful Feeble-mind from his grasp.

   C. The travelers enjoyed the refreshment of the inn for two months.

   D. During this time, two weddings took place.

      i. Christiana's oldest son, Matthew, married Mercy.

      ii. Christiana's second-oldest son, James, married Gaius' daughter Phebe.

   E. After this happy season, the growing band of pilgrims began making their way toward Vanity Fair.

STUDY QUESTIONS

1. _____ found a way to heal Christiana's son from an illness.
   a. Mr. Honest
   b. Great-heart
   c. Interpreter
   d. Mr. Skill

2. As they journeyed on, the pilgrims heard the sound of birds singing lines from the Psalms.
   a. True
   b. False

3. When they reached the Valley of Humiliation, the pilgrims found all of the following except _____.
   a. Apollyon's arrows
   b. A monument commemorating Christian's battle
   c. A desolate wasteland
   d. A shepherd boy

4. Great-heart defeated a giant named Slay-good in the Valley of the Shadow of Death.
   a. True
   b. False

5. On the way to Gaius' inn, the pilgrims enjoyed the company of _____.
   a. The innkeeper's daughter
   b. Mr. Honesty
   c. Feeble-mind
   d. The innkeeper himself

BIBLE STUDY AND DISCUSSION QUESTIONS

1. How was Christiana's son healed after eating the harmful fruit? What kind of medicine did he receive? Why is it meaningful that this took place in the Palace Beautiful?

2. When did the pilgrims see Great-heart again? What does that teach us about prayer?

3. When we were introduced to the Valley of Humiliation in part one, it was as a place of spiritual warfare. What else do we learn about that valley in this message? What kinds of experiences have you had in the Valley of Humiliation?

4. Who was Mr. Fearing? Did he complete his journey to the Celestial City? What instruction and encouragement can his story offer to Christians today?

17

From Vanity
to Doubting Castle

MESSAGE INTRODUCTION

Though there are often points of similarity between the experiences and struggles of believers, each person engages certain spiritual realities differently. For instance, Christian and his other family members spent time in Vanity and visited Doubting Castle; they covered the same ground but were called to act differently and face distinct challenges. In this message we will observe what happened to Christiana and the boys in these places, taking note of Bunyan's rich theology of spiritual warfare.

SCRIPTURE READING

2 Corinthians 10:3-5

TEACHING OBJECTIVES

1. To celebrate faithful Christian witness in adverse settings.
2. To demonstrate how opposition can fuel the growth of the church.
3. To illustrate the constancy of spiritual warfare.
4. To exhort Christians to take bold action against evil spiritual strongholds.

QUOTATION

"Melt the clouds of sin and sadness;
Drive the dark of doubt away;
Giver of immortal gladness,
Fill us with the light of day!"

–Henry van Dyke

LECTURE OUTLINE

I.   The Church in Vanity

   A. Christiana and her company entered the city of Vanity, and they stayed in the home
       of Mr. Mnason.
       i.   Mr. Mnason was an old disciple, and he introduced the pilgrims to several
            other God-fearing residents of Vanity.
            1.   They met Mr. Contrite, Mr. Holy-man, Mr. Love-saints, Mr. Dare-not-lie,
                 and Mr. Penitent.
            2.   They also became acquainted with Mr. Mnason's family.
       ii. During their time in Vanity, Christiana's younger sons, Samuel and
            Joseph, married Mr. Mnason's daughters Grace and Martha.
   B. The city of Vanity was no longer as hostile to pilgrims as it had been in Christian's
       day.
       i.   This change perhaps reflects the decreasing number of English martyrs in
            the 1680s.
       ii. However, there were still evil creatures and things near Vanity.
   C. When a seven-headed monster emerged from the woods and killed several towns-
       people, Great-heart pursued it and mortally wounded it.
   D. After paying their respects to Faithful at the site of his martyrdom, the pilgrims left
       Vanity and followed the highway toward the Delectable Mountains.

II. Storming Doubting Castle

   A. When the pilgrims drew near to By-path Meadow, Great-heart, Mr. Honest, and
       the four boys decided to put an end to the evil of Doubting Castle.
   B. They put Giant Despair and his wife to death, and then they proceeded to raze the
       castle to the ground.
   C. When they returned to the others, bringing with them captives they had freed
       from Despair's dungeon, they had a joyful celebration.
   D. The pilgrims' exploits against beasts and giants illustrate the constant role of spiri-
       tual warfare in the Christian life.

STUDY QUESTIONS

   1. What kind of reception did the pilgrims receive in Vanity?
       a. They were locked in the same cage that once held Christian
       b. The shopkeepers repeatedly urged them to buy things
       c. They were welcomed by God-fearing citizens
       d. The townspeople drove the pilgrims out of the city

   2. Christiana experienced less hostility in Vanity than Christian had.
       a. True
       b. False

3. Great-heart responded to the monster's attack on Vanity by _____ .
   a. Killing it during the attack
   b. Establishing a hospital for the wounded
   c. Descending into the water and going through the river
   d. Pursuing and crippling the monster

4. The four boys did not want to go near Doubting Castle because they were afraid of Giant Despair.
   a. True
   b. False

5. After slaying Giant Despair, the pilgrims _____ .
   a. Destroyed his castle
   b. Gave the released prisoners control of the castle
   c. Held a lavish banquet inside Doubting Castle
   d. Converted the castle into a hostel for travelers

BIBLE STUDY AND DISCUSSION QUESTIONS

1. How did Christiana's experience in Vanity differ from Christian's experience there? In what ways was the power of the gospel revealed in that city?

2. As was demonstrated in Vanity, even a small Christian community can have a considerable effect upon those around them. In what ways have you seen or heard of positive change coming about through faithful Christian witness?

3. What do you think of the decision to attack Giant Despair? What can this story teach us about overcoming doubt and despair?

4. You have probably noticed that part two of this story contains many more battle accounts than part one did. How have these incidents influenced your understanding of spiritual warfare?

18

On to Enchanted Ground

MESSAGE INTRODUCTION

Christiana and her fellow pilgrims draw steadily nearer to the Celestial City. As they journey through the Delectable Mountains, Enchanted Ground, and Beulah Land, they continue to encounter both spiritual opponents and spiritual allies. As their company grows and as they draw ever nearer to the city gates, Christiana is aware that she is nearly at the end of her journey.

SCRIPTURE READING

2 Timothy 4:6-8

TEACHING OBJECTIVES

1. To present several pictures of a faithful Christian life.
2. To describe the enemies of truth.
3. To equip Christians to stand valiantly for God's truth.
4. To remind believers that one day they will be called into the king's presence.

QUOTATION

"Hobgoblin nor foul fiend
Can daunt his spirit;
He knows he at the end
Shall life inherit.
Then fancies fly away,
He'll not fear what men say;
He'll labor night and day
To be a pilgrim."

–Mr. Valiant-for-Truth

LECTURE OUTLINE

I. Lessons from the Shepherds

    A. Arriving at the Delectable Mountains, the pilgrims received a kind welcome from the shepherds who dwelled there.

    B. After providing food and lodging for the travelers, the shepherds showed them several noteworthy sights.

        i. On Mount Marvel they saw a man who knocked mountains down with his words (Mark 11:23).

        ii. On Mount Innocence they watched two men cast dirt upon a godly man, but his white garment was not soiled by the dirt.

        iii. On Mount Charity they saw a man make clothing for the poor, and his materials never ran out.

II. Zeal for Truth

    A. As they left the Delectable Mountains, the pilgrims met a man named Mr. Valiant-for-Truth.

        i. Valiant-for-Truth had been born in the Dark Land and had become a pilgrim after hearing about Christian's journey.

        ii. The others found him after he had defeated three men who were trying to keep him from reaching the Celestial City.

    B. As this man's battle showed, those who stand for truth will be called upon to fight difficult battles.

        i. The first opponent, Wild-head, was headstrong and chaotic.

        ii. The second opponent, Inconsiderate, closed his mind to reason.

        iii. The third opponent, Pragmatic, was opinionated and dictatorial.

    C. Valiant-for-Truth fought well because he had an excellent weapon.

        i. The Jerusalem sword had originated in God's city.

        ii. Never growing blunt, it could penetrate flesh, bones, soul, and spirit.

    D. Valiant-for-Truth recognized that his battle was against the world, the flesh, and the devil.

III. A Summons to Glory

    A. The pilgrims continued to Enchanted Ground and into Beulah Land.

    B. As they drew nearer to the Celestial City, a courier came bearing a letter for Christiana.

        i. She realized that she was being summoned to the city and would soon cross the River of Death.

        ii. She began preparing herself for the crossing and said appropriate words of parting to each of her companions.

    C. On the appointed day, Christiana entered the river, and her pilgrimage was complete.

STUDY QUESTIONS

1. When Christiana and the boys arrived at the Delectable Mountains, the shepherds showed them the same sights that they had shown to Christian.
    a. True
    b. False

2. On Mount Innocence the pilgrims saw _____.
    a. Blind victims of Giant Despair
    b. A man whose garment remained white
    c. A man making clothes for the poor
    d. Someone who would move mountains by speaking to them

3. The pilgrims came upon Mr. Valiant-for-Truth after he had been fighting _____.
    a. The Vanity town militia
    b. Two ruffians sent by Beelzebub
    c. The last remaining giant in Beulah land
    d. Wild-head, Inconsiderate, and Pragmatic

4. What kind of weapon did Valiant-for-Truth use?
    a. A sling and five stones
    b. All-prayer
    c. A Jerusalem sword
    d. A donkey's jawbone

5. Christiana learned that she would enter the Celestial City before any of her traveling companions.
    a. True
    b. False

BIBLE STUDY AND DISCUSSION QUESTIONS

1. The company of pilgrims included not only brave warriors like Great-heart but also several with weaker faith, such as Feeble-mind, Despondency, and Much-afraid. What does this variety in the church communicate about God?

2. Where did Mr. Valiant-for-Truth come from? What led him to become a pilgrim? Why is this significant?

3. What can Mr. Valiant-for-Truth teach us about spiritual warfare? In what ways might God be calling you to stand up for truth?

4. What kind of letter did Christiana receive in Beulah land? What does it mean for a believer to receive this kind of letter?

19

On to the Celestial City

MESSAGE INTRODUCTION

Christiana and her companions have reached the River of Death, but they do not all cross the river at the same time. This reflects the actual experiences of believers. Just as God raises up new disciples, He also calls His people to one day depart this life and join Him. In this final message of our study, we will learn about the final days of many of the pilgrims we have met so far. In their stories, we can find hope and wisdom to live well and to be ready when our Lord calls us to His side.

SCRIPTURE READINGS

Isaiah 43:1-7; 1 Thessalonians 4:13-14

TEACHING OBJECTIVES

1. To describe the process of departing from this life.
2. To celebrate the hope that awaits God's people.
3. To remind Christ's followers that they do not need to fear death.
4. To encourage Christians to prepare themselves for their eventual death, so that they might live well and die well.

QUOTATION

"Thro' many dangers, toils, and snares,
I have already come;
'Tis grace hath brought me safe thus far,
And grace will lead me home."

–John Newton

LECTURE OUTLINE

I. Eternal Rest for Weary Pilgrims

A. Shortly after Christiana received her summons to the Celestial City, Mr. Ready-to-halt was called to the city, and he bequeathed his crutches to his son.

B. Mr. Despondency was called next.

i. He had dealt with melancholy his whole life.

ii. He and his daughter, Much-afraid, were eager to be free from fear and despair.

iii. They did not bequeath their melancholy to anyone.

C. One by one, each of the pilgrims was taken, until only Christiana's sons and their families remained.

II. The Climax of Life

A. In contemporary society, death is unknown, mysterious, and feared.

i. Increased life expectancy has largely pushed death back into old age.

ii. People tend to die alone and out of sight.

B. In contrast, death was familiar to Bunyan and his original readers.

i. Death was a common occurrence, and it could happen even to the young.

ii. Most people had spent time with the dying and had been present with someone at the moment of death.

C. A person's last words would often be written down and preserved.

i. Christiana's final words were, "I come, Lord, to be with thee and bless thee."

ii. Mr. Ready-to-halt uttered, "Welcome, life."

iii. Mr. Feeble-mind ended with, "Hold out faith and patience."

iv. Mr. Despondency exclaimed, "Farewell, night; welcome, day!"

v. Mr. Valiant-for-Truth cried, "Death, where is thy sting? Grave, where is thy victory?"

vi. Mr. Standfast said, "Take me, for I come unto thee."

D. Each departure was marked by joyful celebration.

III. A Parting Question

A. As Bunyan brings this story to an end, his readers are left with the great evangelical question: Are you ready to die?

B. In order to answer this question in the affirmative, one must understand and embrace the gospel, which is present throughout this story.

C. As this study draws to a close, we would do well to read Bunyan's masterpiece and profit from it.

STUDY QUESTIONS

1. No longer needing them, Mr. Ready-to-halt burned his crutches when he entered the Celestial City.

a. True

b. False

2. When Mr. Despondency was called to go to the Celestial City, he _____ .
    a. Bequeathed his melancholy to Mr. Feeble-mind
    b. Began to despair because he feared death
    c. Was joined by his daughter
    d. Stopped having nightmares about being Giant Despair's prisoner

3. Dr. Thomas mentioned that in Bunyan's day it was common to _____ .
    a. Prepare a lavish feast for a dying person
    b. Place the elderly in institutions where they would die out of sight
    c. Reach old age without ever seeing someone die
    d. Write down a person's final words

4. What were Mr. Valiant-for-Truth's final words?
    a. "Goodbye, everyone"
    b. "Death, where is thy sting? Grave, where is thy victory?"
    c. "Let us cross over the river and rest in the shade of the trees"
    d. "It is finished"

5. The message of the gospel does not just appear at the end of *Pilgrim's Progress*, but is present throughout the story.
    a. True
    b. False

BIBLE STUDY AND DISCUSSION QUESTIONS

1. In contrast to part 1, many of the pilgrims remained on the other side of the river for a long time before crossing over to the Celestial City. Why would Bunyan end the story in this way? What does this element of the story say about the calling of Christians in this present life?

2. Because of Christian's faith, his family went in one generation from being an unbelieving family to being a family with a Christian heritage. What hope does this offer for lost or broken homes today?

3. Which of the characters in this story do you most identify with? How has God used this study to teach you more about yourself and your own journey of faith?

4. If God were to call you to go to Him now, would you be ready?